HOW TO IMPROVE AT PLAYING THE
GUITAR

Tom Clark

CONTENTS

INTRODUCTION

The guitar is the world's most popular instrument, perhaps because of its portability and adaptability to a vast range of musical styles. This book will help you improve your playing, from learning about the basics to writing your own melodies. In the words of Harlan Howard, all you need is 'three chords and the truth', so let's get going!

A BIT OF HISTORY

The origins of the guitar are lost in the mists of time but, one thing is sure, that it was adapted from older instruments, such as the Moroccan 'oud' and the Scandinavian 'lute'. The earliest guitars first appeared around 1600 and had 10 strings, arranged in five pairs. Steel-string acoustic guitars were first developed in the 19th century and the first electric guitars were built in the 1940s.

HOW TO USE THIS BOOK

You can work through the book page-by-page or leap forward to learn about a particular skill or practise playing some exercises. Step-by-step guides help you get to grips with techniques and the exercises help you master them.

Wizard Boxes

Look out for the helpful boxes, which will give you tons of juicy extras including top tips on technique, and explanations of the terms, signs and symbols used in guitar-playing and music.

THE GUITAR

Before you start playing, it makes sense to get to know your instrument. A guitar is not a complicated musical instrument and, even though there are many different types of guitar, they all share the same basic working parts.

THE GUITAR FAMILY

Not counting banjos, ukeleles, mandolins and all the other instruments in the family, there is a mind-boggling variety of guitars. Luckily, however, they divide neatly into two different types – acoustic guitars and electric guitars.

Guitar varieties

Acoustic guitars all make sound in the same way – when you pluck a string, the sound is amplified (made louder) inside a hollow soundbox. Classical guitars with their nylon strings and wide fretboards are the ideal guitar for beginners. Steel-string guitars tend to be bigger and boxier than classical guitars, with slimmer necks. There are no strict rules, but classical guitars are mostly used to play classical and Spanish flamenco music, while steel-string guitars feature in folk, jazz and rock music.

Electric guitars use electric gizmos called 'pick-ups' to amplify the sound. Because they don't rely on a soundbox to create their sound, they are often solid bodied (*see* box).

Going Electric

Electric guitars use 'pick-ups' to make their sound. Pick-ups convert the vibration of the steel strings into electrical signals. Unplugged, an electric guitar doesn't make much noise... but you can make a much, much louder sound when you play it through an 'amplifier'. Amplifiers take the weak signals from the pick-ups and boost them to ear-splitting levels.

Effects Pedals

There are any number of things that you can do with the signal from an electric guitar. Effects pedals are electronics circuits that change the way the guitar sounds. 'Distortion' adds volume and crunch, while 'delay' makes endless repeating echoes.

Guitar Lead

As well as an amplifier, the one other piece of equipment essential for playing the electric guitar is a lead. This cord connects the guitar to the amplifier – without it, no sound.

4

PARTS OF A GUITAR

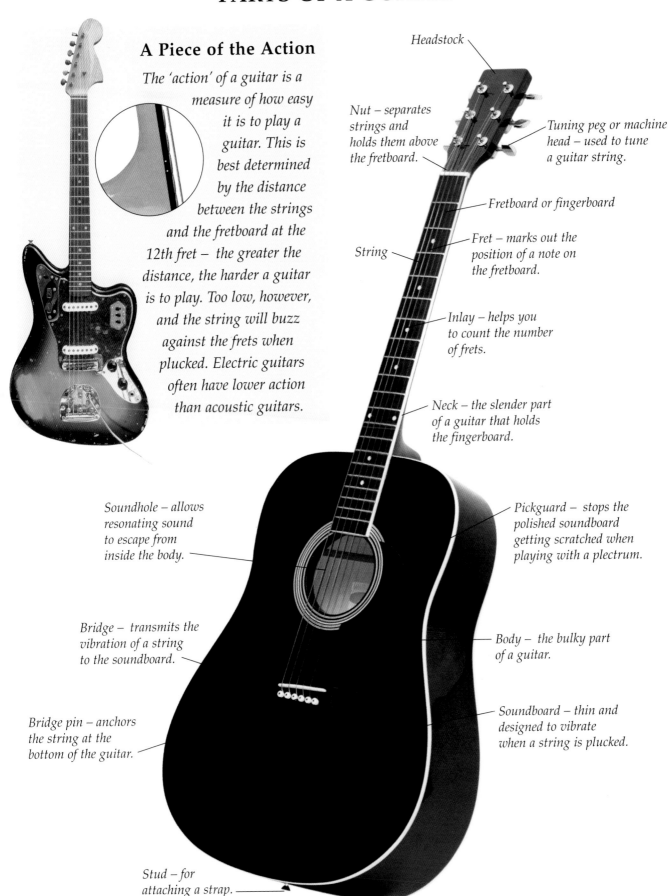

A Piece of the Action

The 'action' of a guitar is a measure of how easy it is to play a guitar. This is best determined by the distance between the strings and the fretboard at the 12th fret – the greater the distance, the harder a guitar is to play. Too low, however, and the string will buzz against the frets when plucked. Electric guitars often have lower action than acoustic guitars.

Headstock

Nut – separates strings and holds them above the fretboard.

Tuning peg or machine head – used to tune a guitar string.

Fretboard or fingerboard

String

Fret – marks out the position of a note on the fretboard.

Inlay – helps you to count the number of frets.

Neck – the slender part of a guitar that holds the fingerboard.

Soundhole – allows resonating sound to escape from inside the body.

Pickguard – stops the polished soundboard getting scratched when playing with a plectrum.

Bridge – transmits the vibration of a string to the soundboard.

Body – the bulky part of a guitar.

Soundboard – thin and designed to vibrate when a string is plucked.

Bridge pin – anchors the string at the bottom of the guitar.

Stud – for attaching a strap.

TUNING

Before you can play anything on your guitar, you must tune it. Each string is tuned to a specific note so that the guitar doesn't sound jarring and 'off-key' when you play it.

E A D G B E

STANDARD TUNING

The usual tuning for a guitar is from 6th string to 1st string (*see* opposite page): E, A, D, G, B, E. This is called standard tuning (there are other ways of tuning a guitar) and a good way to remember it is with the silly sentence, 'Edward And David Grow Big Elephants'.

TUNING *TO* SOMETHING

Guitars can be 'tuned to themselves', so that each string sounds in tune with the others, but if you are going to play with other people, it's a good idea to tune all the instruments to the same note. A tuning fork or pitch pipes can give a reference note (for example an A note of 440 Hz), but an electronic tuner detects the sound of each individual string and tells you whether it's in tune or not. Some tuners will even tell you which way to turn the tuning peg to get a string in tune.

Technical Terms

PITCH – The 'lowness' or 'highness' of a guitar string, or note, is called its pitch.

Electronic tuner

HOW TO TUNE UP

Every string is wound around a 'tuning peg' (for classical guitars) or 'machine head' (for steel-string guitars). To adust the tuning, these are turned to make the string tighter (makes the pitch higher) or looser (makes the pitch lower). It's always good to check your tuning before playing because strings can go out of tune quickly.

SIMPLE TUNING METHOD

Once your 6th string is in tune, you can use it to tune the rest of the strings.

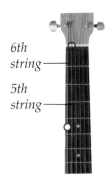

6th string

5th string

1

Play an A on the 5th fret of the 6th string. Now play the open 5th string and turn the tuning peg until both strings are in tune with each other.

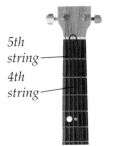

5th string

4th string

2

Play a D note on the 5th fret of the 5th string. Play the open 4th string and match the sounds.

Top Tip

It's always easier to tune 'up' to a note than tuning 'down'. Don't give up if it is hard at first – tuning takes practice.

3

Repeat the process playing a G on the 5th fret of the 4th string and the open 3rd string.

4

This time play a B note on the 4th fret of the 3rd string and compare it to the open 2nd string.

5

Finally, the 5th fret of the 2nd string will give you another E note, to which you can tune the open 1st string.

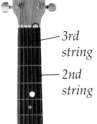

4th string

3rd string

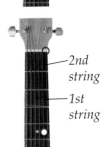

3rd string

2nd string

2nd string

1st string

7

PLAYING POSITIONS

You should feel comfortable when you play the guitar and learning a good playing position will help you relax and snag those hard-to-reach notes.

There are two main ways of holding a guitar: a 'folk' style has it resting on your leg on the same side as your strumming or picking hand. In this position the neck is horizontal. In a 'classical' playing style, the guitar rests on the opposite knee to the plucking hand. The neck slopes upwards in this position. Many players use a footstool to make it more comfortable.

Folk style

Classical playing position

STRUMMING AND PICKING

To make any sound on a guitar, you need to pluck the strings. You can do this one at a time, which is called 'picking', or all together, which is called 'strumming'. Get ready to raise the roof.

STRUMMING TECHNIQUE

1

You can strum with your thumb, but it's better to learn to use a plectrum. A plectrum, or pick, is a small plastic triangle. Plucking the strings with it makes a strong, clear and even tone. Grip it loosely between thumb and index finger, and point it in towards the guitar body.

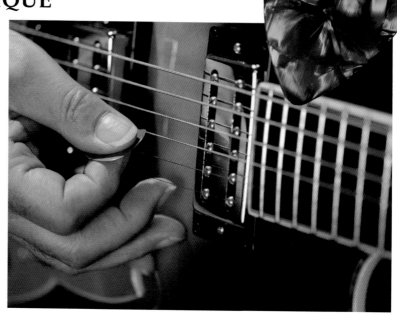

2

Your elbow should be resting comfortably on the guitar and your hand is off the strings.

3

Gently brush the plectrum down across the strings, taking care to hit each string cleanly one at a time.

4

Make sure to strum midway between the bridge and the top of the body. This makes the loudest sound.

5

As your hand moves down, rotate your wrist away from the guitar body to complete the stroke.

This is rather oddly called the 'upstroke', since you are playing notes going up the scale.

6

The downstroke
is the reverse
of the upstroke.

7

Start slowly
and concentrate
on accuracy before
building up speed.

*Although your hand travels upwards,
this stroke is called the 'downstroke'.*

Top Tip

*When it comes to strumming, the harder
you strum the worse it sounds. Make sure
you brush the strings gently and evenly.*

PLAYING P-I-M-A

Classical guitar is played by plucking individual
strings with the thumb or a finger. The thumb
plays downwards, while the fingers push
through the string and in towards the palm
of the hand. Do not pull the strings outwards.
In classical guitar, each playing digit is given
a letter. The thumb is 'p', the 1st finger is 'i',
the 2nd finger is 'm' and the 3rd finger is 'a'.
This labelling system has the advantage
of allowing a composer to show the picking
pattern on a piece of music.

Classical Strokes

*There are two types of finger stroke in the
classical right-hand technique. Rest stroke
('apoyando') produces a fuller, more singing
and projected tone, suitable for melodic lines.
Free stroke ('tirando') is used for more
intricate plucking patterns. With apoyando,
the thumb or finger
comes to rest on the
next-door string.
With tirando,
the finger or
thumb finishes
above the strings.*

9

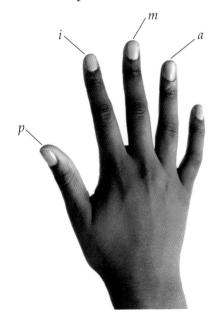

MUSICAL NOTATION

Guitar has its own special method for writing down tunes, called 'tablature'. 'Tab' is really quick and easy to read, but it's also worth taking the time to learn how to read 'standard notation' – what you might call 'reading music'.

HOW TAB WORKS

Tablature is a really simple way of writing down guitar music. Each line represents a string on your guitar. The numbers correspond to the fret number on the fingerboard.

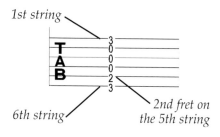

1st string

6th string

2nd fret on the 5th string

1

This is tab for the chord of G major. When the numbers are in a vertical line, it means play them all together.

2

The tab lines represent the strings of the guitar and show you which frets to finger.

3

The player's fingers match the positions shown on the tab.

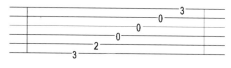

4

When the notes of a chord are staggered, it means they are played separately, as an 'arpeggio'.

STANDARD NOTATION

In standard notation, notes are written on a 'stave'. Every note on a guitar fretboard has its own unique place on the stave. Standard notation is more versatile than tablature because it's easier to note more complex rhythms and finger patterns for plucking.

5

Single-note sequences are written one after the other, reading from left to right.

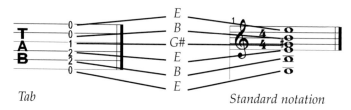

Tab

Standard notation

PRACTICE PIECES

Practise reading tablature and playing along with the three examples below. Once you have got the hang of tablature, try to get a feel for how the notes on the stave correspond to the fret positions on your guitar fingerboard. Test yourself by covering the tab with a piece of paper and seeing if you can still play along. Remember to start off playing slowly before building speed.

BLUES SCALES EXERCISE

This exercise uses notes from the blues scale (*see* page 36).

MAJOR PENTATONIC EXERCISE

You will find the major pentatonic scale in its entirety on page 38.

MINOR PENTATONIC EXERCISE

The minor pentatonic scale is often used by rock guitarists when they play solos. Here is an exercise based on notes from the scale (*see* page 39).

WARMING UP

Just like any sports person, if you want to perform well, you're going to have to warm up first. Here are some tips and tricks to get your blood pumping.

Practise Clever

Warming up before playing is very important. As well as loosening the fingers, it gets you focused and ready for whatever you need to do. Here are some tips for warming up:

- *Begin your practice with slow and rhythmic playing, giving your fingers a chance to warm up gradually.*
- *Pick different warm-up exercises for each practice.*
- *Once you can play the warm-ups, challenge yourself to play them faster. Try them out 0both staccato and legato (see page 27).*

BLUES SCALES EXERCISE

This blues scale is in the key of G major. This means it is based around the notes in the chord of G (right).

G

UP THE NECK IN OCTAVES

Try this ascending octaves exercise to build up your speed, agility and accuracy. Keep the notes clean and even.

MY OWN WARM-UP EXERCISE

This is the exercise I use to warm up before going on stage. Note how the note length gets shorter in the final two bars (it speeds up, but the notes stay evenly spaced). Now you could call this noodling!

Now try this warm-up routine. It starts on the 7th fret of the 6th string – which is a B note (shown left).

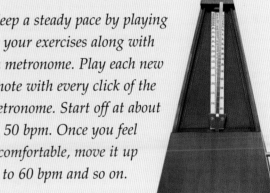

March to the Beat

Keep a steady pace by playing your exercises along with a metronome. Play each new note with every click of the metronome. Start off at about 50 bpm. Once you feel comfortable, move it up to 60 bpm and so on.

EXERCISE 13.1

This is another single-note sequence, which ends on a D note – 5th fret on the 5th string (*see* right). Pay careful attention to the rhythm and notice how the different 'note values' affect it (*see* page 18).

EXERCISE 13.2

OPEN CHORDS

Chords are combinations of two or more notes played at the same time. Open chords use the tuning of the open (unfretted) guitar strings to create chiming chords. It only takes a small number of chords to unlock a vast wealth of songs.

CHORD CHARTS

When playing chords, try to keep a good hand position, with your thumb planted firmly on the middle of the neck, a nice rounded hand shape and your fingers pressing down squarely on the frets.

MAJOR CHORDS

Chords that are made from the major scale have a 'happy' feel. This is because the 'intervals' (gaps between the notes) in the major scale always make the perfect harmonic sound.

> ### Chords at Your Fingertips
> *Use these pages as a chord dictionary – you can flip back to them any time you need to remember a certain chord shape.*

E MAJOR

E major is made up of the notes E, B, E, G#, B and E. Play all six strings together.

A MAJOR

A major is formed from the notes A, E, A, C# and E. Make sure to play only the top five strings.

D MAJOR

D major uses only the top four strings. It's made up of the notes D, A, D and F#.

G MAJOR

You can play all six strings for G major. The chord uses the notes G, B, D, G, B and G.

14

C MAJOR

Be careful to tuck your fourth finger out of the way to avoid deadening the 6th string.

F MAJOR

The chord of F major involves a 'half-barre', in which the 1st finger frets the 1st fret on both the 1st and 2nd string.

MINOR CHORDS

Based on the notes of the minor scales, minor chords have a wistful, melancholic feel. Try playing a major chord of any key, followed by a minor chord in the same key to hear the difference.

Roots and Tonics

Chords are made of combinations of notes from the scale in that key. For example, E major chord is made of notes from the E major scale. The first note of the scale is called the 'tonic'. In most open chords the 'root' note (the lowest note) is also the tonic.

E MINOR (Em)

The notes E, B, E, G, B and E make up the chord of E minor, which is played on all six strings.

A MINOR (Am)

Like all minor chords, A major is made by dropping the third note in the scale a semitone – a half tone, or one fret.

Super Strength

The more you play, the stronger your fingers will get. With practice your muscles will get harder, your fingers will toughen up and your chords will sound much better for it.

D MINOR (Dm)

D minor is played on the top four strings – the notes of D, A, D and F.

SEVENTH CHORDS

Seventh chords are a special group of chords that, along with the notes of the major or minor scale, also have an added 'dominant seventh'. This is the seventh note in the scale and is a whole tone (or two frets down), from the root note, or 'tonic ' (*see* box, page 15).

E7

Lifting the 3rd finger when playing an E major chord gives you an E7. You can also try fretting the 3rd on the 2nd string.

G7

The fingering of G7 is quite different to G major. Try fretting the 1st-string G with your 4th finger to make a swift change.

D7

Like all D open chords, D7 is only played on the top four strings. D7 is made up of D, A, C and F#.

Am7

Am7 is made by lifting up the 3rd finger – you can try the same trick to turn an E minor into an Em7.

Seventh chords have a cool, 'blues-y' feel – try playing A major and following it up with an A7.

C7

The seventh note in the C major scale is easily dropped in to the chord of C major.

Clean Chords

Avoid buzzing notes by pressing down on the strings as hard as you can and getting close up to the fret. 'Bunch' your fingers together to stop deadening the open strings.

Dm7

The Dm7 chord, like F major, is played with a half-barre on the top two strings, made with the 1st finger.

CHORDS AND SINGLE NOTES

By now, you have excelled at the skills of plucking and strumming with a plectrum, and coped admirably with the hardships of fretting open chords. Now it's time to try combining the two…

THE IMPORTANCE OF PRACTICE

An essential skill for any guitar player is the ability to move smoothly between chords and single notes. Once you master the technique, you will be able to beat out rhythm, accompaniment and solo melody lines, as well as intricate fills and riffs to spice up your solid chord foundation. Sadly, there is no substitute for practice. The only way of making sure that when you change between chords and single notes it all flows properly, is to spend as much time as you can practising the techniques on your guitar.

In this exercise, a bar of chords is followed by two bars of melody line. Try your best to 'flow' smoothly from the chords to the single-note movement. Imagine switching lanes on a motorway – keeping the same speed you shoot off in another direction, without even braking.

EXERCISE 17.1

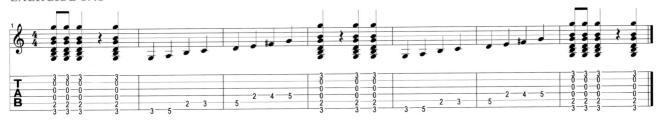

Here is a similar exercise in the key of G major (based around the chord and scale of G major). The changes happen a little more often in this piece. Look out for the chord rhythms.

EXERCISE 17.2

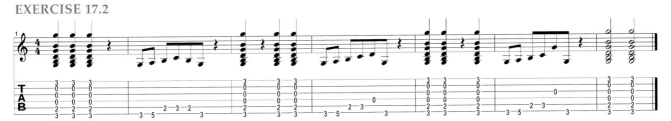

RHYTHM

Rhythm is at the heart of all music – it is the beat that keeps a song rolling along and sets your foot tappin'. It can become very complex, but always at the root of rhythm are notes and beats of varying lengths.

YOU GOT RHYTHM

The secret of good rhythm is knowing your note values. Different notes last for different lengths of time (*see* box). One of the big advantages that standard musical notation has over tablature is that it is much easier to show the rhythm you play, which is why we have included both forms for you in this book. As always, the best way to learn is to give it a try.

Note Values

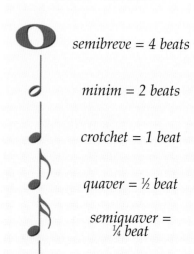

semibreve = 4 beats

minim = 2 beats

crotchet = 1 beat

quaver = ½ beat

semiquaver = ¼ beat

dotted minim = 3 beats

dotted crotchet = 1½ beats

dotted quaver = ¾ beats

1

Clap this rhythm first (*see* above). Pay close attention to the lengths of each note.

2

If whole melodies were written out in one long line, it would get pretty confusing, so notes are grouped into 'bars' containing the same number of beats. Practise clapping the rhythm above.

MUSICAL STYLES

No other instrument – with perhaps the exception of the piano – adapts itself to so many different musical styles as the guitar. It really is a chameleon instrument, taking in everything from classical to jazz, Latin and world music.

CLASSICAL AND FLAMENCO

The Spanish guitar, with its small body and nylon strings, is used for classical playing and traditional Latin styles of music, including many types of Latin-American and Caribbean music. The guitar tends to be a rhythm instrument in styles such as 'bossa nova' (Brazilian jazz) or salsa, but a lead instrument for classical compositions. The flamboyant Spanish style called 'flamenco' also uses a classical guitar, with added 'tap' plates on the soundboard for striking.

BLUES AND JAZZ

The steel-string acoustic guitar is the main instrument of blues and jazz, as well as folk and country music. It is often played on its own, as a rhythm instrument. Blues players often use their palm to mute the strings (*see* page 21), creating a 'shuffle' rhythm.

Many blues guitarists play 'slide guitar', using a metal or glass 'slide' on the strings to make a wailing, or moaning sound.

The 'arch-top' semi-acoustic guitar is a great favourite with jazz musicians for its warm, mellow tones.

BASIC PLUCKING

The techniques for plucking the guitar strings are derived from classical music, but they have been adapted to fit a whole range of music styles. To build up your fluency, you should begin with just your thumb and first finger.

FINGER-PICKIN' GOOD

A good hand position is essential to achieve accuracy and agility, but even so there are different styles of plucking.

1

Start off with this simple exercise, which will get your fingers used to the feeling of picking individual strings.

Classical style – with the guitar on the left leg, the arm has the space to arch around the guitar body. The hand is rounded, relaxed and away from the strings.

Folk style – the guitar is held more horizontally (often on the right leg) and is therefore much tighter to the body. The hand is flatter and closer to the strings, ready to mute them with the palm if needed.

MALAGUEÑA

Malagueña is a traditional Spanish folk tune, based around the chords of E and Am. Start slowly and concentrate on getting the notes right before you aim for speed.

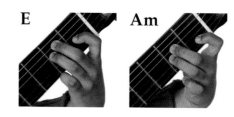

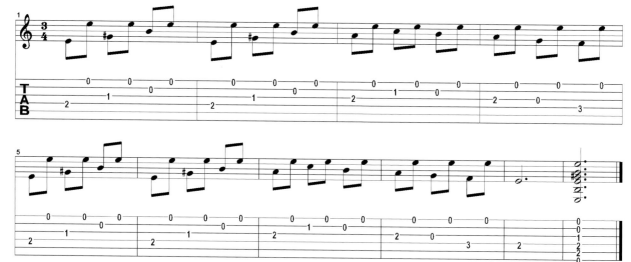

PALM MUTING

By 'damping' the strings, palm muting stops the notes ringing out. While it may sound like a strange thing to do to a guitar, this technique can add a whole world of tension and dynamics to your playing.

HOW TO PALM MUTE

Something in the way? When you play palm muted, the guitar makes a 'thunky', deadened sound. It works particularly well when playing chords with a plectrum or with country-style fingerpicking.

1

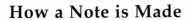

Rest the flat of your playing hand across all the strings, as close to the bridge as possible. Pick any note with a plectrum to hear the effect.

2

Play a chord with the strings muted. 'Accent' the first few notes to get a really good 'thunk'. Experiment with your hand position and with fingerpicking.

How a Note is Made

A normal, unmuted note on a guitar is made by plucking the string. This makes the string vibrate (usually in an up-and-down-motion). On an acoustic guitar, the vibration of the string is picked up at the bridge, and transmitted by the bridge making the soundboard – the front face of the guitar – vibrate. Now you have a much bigger thing vibrating, so the sound of a single string is amplified. The sound resonating inside the body of the guitar also increases the volume.

Different kinds of strings make different sounds – classical guitars are strung with soft-sounding nylon strings, steel-string acoustics use bright-sounding, round-wound steel, while jazzers prefer the duller, flat-wound strings.

MAJOR AND MINOR SCALES

The major and minor scales are the two most important systems in Western music. Both scales have an easily recognizable 'feel' and most tunes are made using the combinations of notes, chords and harmonies that are found in them.

MAJOR SCALE

If you want to write a happy or bright sounding melody, you would tend to use the major scale.

C MAJOR SCALE

Positions

Because any note can be found on any string, scales and chords can be played in several different positions on the guitar fingerboard. The first fret is called '1st position', second fret '2nd position' and so forth.

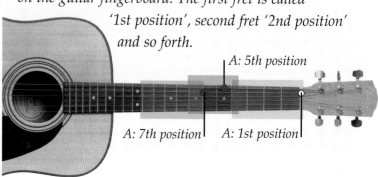

A: 5th position

A: 7th position   A: 1st position

NATURAL MINOR SCALE

The natural minor scale is a sad sounding scale – the third note, sixth note and seventh note of the scale have been 'flattened' (dropped by one fret, or a semitone) to create a darker sound. A minor is the related minor key to C major – compare the two scales to see their similarities and hear their differences.

Top Tip

Playing scales also doubles up as a really good warm-up activity and a way of increasing your speed on the fingerboard.

22

PLAY-ALONG SONGS

Let's put into practice all the things you have learned so far. Here are three simple melodies to get you working on your chords, single notes, pick-work and fingerstyle. See if you can guess which melodies are major and which are minor.

MELODIES FOR PLAYING ALONG

Use the melodies below to put everything you have learnt into practice. For example, play with a plectrum and then move on to fingerpicking. Each melody is based around either the major or natural minor scales.

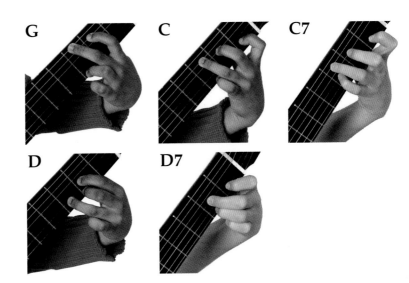

MELODY 23.1

SCARBOROUGH FAIR

A SPOT OF REVISION

O ne of the best things that you can do when learning to play any instrument, is to look back and review what you have learned every now and again. This reinforces your technique and helps things sink in.

CHORD PATTERNS AND MELODIES

With just three chords, such as G major, C major and D major, you can play a huge number of tunes. Try out different combinations of these three chords to see what you come up with – and drop in an A minor to spice things up a little.

Technical Terms

CHORD PROGRESSION –
A regularly repeating pattern of chords is called a 'chord progression'.

G   C   D

Here is a melody that uses the chords of G major, C major and D major. Play it slowly at first and concentrate on revising your skills of moving from chords to single notes.

EXERCISE 24.1

HAMMER-ONS

You can add colour, depth and range to your guitar playing with a few simple effects. 'Hammer-ons' are one of the most important techniques, helping you to connect notes more smoothly. It is time to take things to the next level.

HAMMER TIME

The hammer-on is a percussive technique – using your fingers to beat the fingerboard. It helps you play music smoothly, allowing the notes to flow from one to the next. Hammer-ons are a key technique when it comes to playing melodies or solos (*see* pages 40–41) and also for playing 'legato' (*see* page 27).

Finger Strength

Practising to get your hammer-ons sounding clean and loud is a great way to build up strength in your fingers. Similarly, practising scales and chord progressions will also improve finger strength and make your hammer-ons sound much better.

HOW TO HAMMER ON

1

Fret the 6th fret on the 1st string with your 1st finger. Pluck it and let it ring.

2

While the note is ringing, swing (or 'hammer') your 3rd finger down onto the 8th fret (1st string), as forcefully as you can. You should hear the second note sound.

Hammer-ons in Tab

This is how an instruction to pull-off looks in tablature:

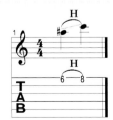

PULL-OFFS

A 'pull-off' is the exact opposite of a hammer-on. Where a hammer-on is a different way of playing an ascending note, pull-offs are for descending runs. Both techniques allow smooth phrasing that cannot be made by picking individual notes.

PULL THE OTHER ONE

In many ways, pull-offs are easier than hammer-ons because it doesn't take as much finger strength to make the sound right.

Pull-offs in Tab

This is how an instruction to pull-off looks in tablature:

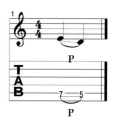

PULL-OFFS TO AN OPEN STRING

1

Fret the 3rd fret on the 5th string with your 2nd finger. You can use any finger for this, but your 2nd is most often your strongest one. Pluck the string.

2

While the note is ringing, pull your finger away from the fretboard forcibly, plucking the string with your fretting finger to make the open A note (2nd string) sound. Practise getting the A to sound cleanly.

PULL-OFFS TO A FRETTED STRING

1

First fret the note on which you want to finish (5th fret, 2nd string in this case). Then play the note two frets above (fretted with the 4th finger).

2

Pull your 3rd finger off, plucking the string to sound the D note (5th fret, 2nd string). Practise adding hammer-ons and pull-offs into a scale (*see* page 22).

LEGATO AND STACCATO

Both these strange-sounding words are ways of introducing 'dynamics', shape and articulation into your playing. They are opposites of each other – 'legato' is a smooth, unhurried style, while 'staccato' is choppy and edgy.

SMOOTH LEGATO

'Legato' connects single notes together, so that they flow with no silence between them. The way to picture legato is like a wave, because a wave always flows without stopping and starting.

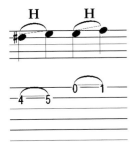

Legato is played using hammer-ons and pull-offs to smooth out the notes, indicated by 'tie-lines'.

CHOPPY STACCATO

'Staccato' notes have silence in between them. You can picture staccato notes as a line of dots because each dot has a space between them.

Staccato notes are indicated by dots above the notes. Think of playing them as if the guitar strings were red hot.

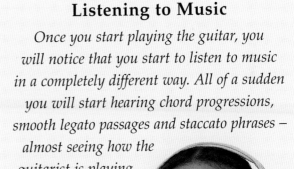

Listening to Music

Once you start playing the guitar, you will notice that you start to listen to music in a completely different way. All of a sudden you will start hearing chord progressions, smooth legato passages and staccato phrases – almost seeing how the guitarist is playing. Hearing music in this way is really good practice. Listen to your favourite songs and see if you can tap along to the beat.

27

BUILDING UP SPEED

As you get more confidence and your finger strength improves, you will want to start increasing the pace at which you play. If you pay attention to getting your basic techniques solid, you will find that speed comes quite easily.

RHYTHM

Page 18 covered note values – showing you how to count bars of three and four beats. We met crotchets (quarter notes) and quavers (eighth notes). Here we are going to cover sixteenth notes which are twice as fast as eighth notes.

Sixteenth notes are called semiquavers. At double the speed of quavers, you get 16 in a bar of 4/4 (four for each beat).

Thrilling Trills

A trill is a fancy 'twiddle' on a note, made by playing a quick succession of semiquaver hammer-ons and pull-offs.

The trill notation

What you play...

This is what semiquavers look like in a 4/4 bar:

EXERCISE 28.1

G

1

Play along with a metronome to get the feel. Set it to a slow speed (say 40 bpm) and concentrate on getting the notes to fall on every beat. Practise with a pick.

2

Increase the speed of the metronome until you can only just get the notes in time. Practise at this speed until it feels easier. Now increase the speed again.

FINGERPICKING

Playing the guitar with your fingers is an incredibly versatile technique. All of a sudden you can provide your own rhythm section while floating a tinkling melody across the upper register – it sure is fingerpickin' good.

FOLK FINGERSTYLE

Getting the correct hand position is essential for fingerstyle.

1

Pull your wrist in so that it is flat on the body of the guitar. Your fingers curl over and your thumb is parallel to the strings. This can feel a little strange at first.

2

Fret a chord and try thumbing the bass notes while picking out the top three notes. Do this until the hand position feels natural. Many players use a thumbpick.

Advanced Techniques

While frowned upon by formal practitioners, taking your thumb from behind the neck and hooking it 'over the top' to fret bass notes, is a very useful weapon to have in your armoury.

Here are a couple of examples to get you started with fingerpicking techniques:

EXERCISE 29.1

EXERCISE 29.2

BARRE CHORDS

Barre chords allow you to play chords anywhere on the neck. The shapes are the same ones that you learned as open chords (*see* pages 14–16), but you use your first finger to create a 'barre', or an artificial nut, across the guitar's neck.

BARRE TECHNIQUE

Barre chords are named by the shape of the open chord that they imitate. Compare the open E major chord with the E-shape barre chord (right).

1

Lay your 1st finger across all the strings. Try to apply even pressure. Your 2nd, 3rd and 4th fingers form the shape of the open chord.

E MAJOR (OPEN CHORD)

The nut forms a 'barre' for the open major chord.

E-SHAPE BARRE CHORD

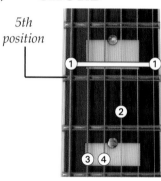

5th position

The 1st finger 'barre' replaces the nut, while the rest of the fingers initates the E shape.

OTHER BARRE CHORDS

E-MINOR-SHAPE

> ### Stick With It
>
> *This is one of the biggest steps in learning to play the guitar and sometimes it can make your fingers sore. Stick with it – as soon as your flexibility and strength increase, this will become second nature.*

A-SHAPE

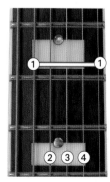

A-MINOR-SHAPE

POWER CHORDS

These useful chords are partial barre chords, made from the first three notes of the barre chord. Since they do not require a barre, they are much easier to play than a full barre chord. Rock guitarists use them a lot because they can shift between them much more quickly. Compare this type of chord to the full barre chords shown on the opposite page.

'A' POWER CHORD

Since they do not contain the third note of the scale, power chords are neither major nor minor.

Practise your power-chord techniques with this melody. Play close attention to the rhythm in bar 5.

EXERCISE 31.1

COMPOSE A MELODY USING BARRE CHORDS

1

Test out your new knowledge by inventing a tune using E-shape and A-shape barre chords. Try to think of chord progressions you have already played in this book – can you play them as barre chords?

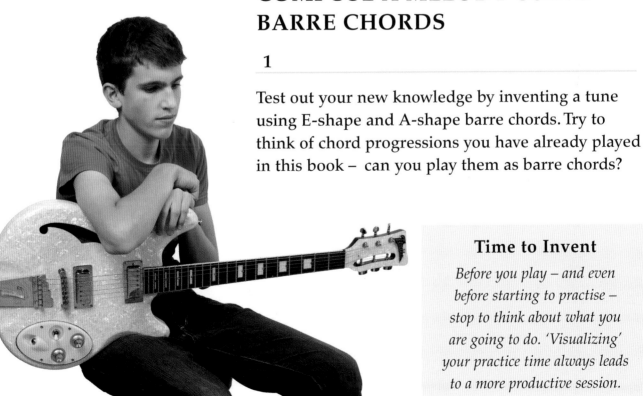

Time to Invent

Before you play – and even before starting to practise – stop to think about what you are going to do. 'Visualizing' your practice time always leads to a more productive session.

MORE SCALES EXERCISES

It is time to revisit the scales. Remember the major scale and natural minor scale on page 22? Well, here are more exercises based on these important scales.

A MAJOR SCALE

Use these scale charts to help you with the exercises.

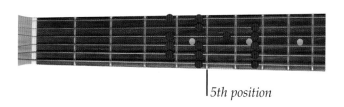

5th position

This exercise takes the scale of A major.

EXERCISE 32.1

A MINOR SCALE

5th position

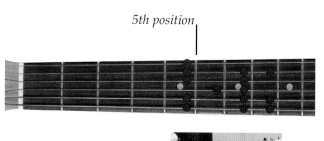

Your starting position for exercise 32.1.

This exercise takes the scale of A minor.

EXERCISE 32.2

Exercise 32.2 starts at the 7th position.

This exercise mixes both A major and A minor scales.

EXERCISE 32.3

Begin exercise 32.3 on the 10th fret.

32

TIME SIGNATURES

Nothing could be more important to rhythm-keeping than 'time signatures'. That is why they are put right at the start of any piece of music. Time signatures tell you how many beats in a bar and how many notes per measure.

The top number tells us how many beats are in the bar.

The bottom number tells us what type of beat it is. A '4' means it is a quarter note (a crotchet) and an '8' means it is an eighth note (a quaver).

Lessons

Lessons are not essential by any means – you can teach yourself an awful lot by using books such as this one. However, as you progress it is sometimes very helpful to have personal attention to help you get through some sticky areas. A guitar teacher can give you a push when you might give up, and it is always great to play with other people!

4/4 TIME SIGNATURE

In a bar of 4/4, there are four quarter beats in every bar. You can have four crotchets, eight quavers or 16 semiquavers. Clap out each bar.

3/4 TIME SIGNATURE

In a bar of 3/4, there are only three quarter beats in the bar. There are many ways of organizing the bar – the last bar of this exercise has a classic 'waltz' beat. Try clapping it.

PLAY-ALONG SONGS

Well done! You have completed this section, where you have battled with barre chords, learned some silky solo skills and hopefully gained a lot more confidence.

TEST YOUR PLAYING

Below are three exercises for you to practise. Test your progress by sightreading the tablature (or standard notation).

G

SIMPLE FINGERPICKING

Keep the tempo of this piece, based around the chord of G major, slow and steady.

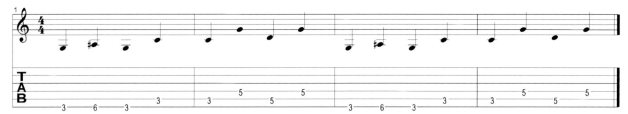

G MAJOR WORKOUT

This piece will test your fingerpicking skills to the max.

NATURAL MINOR MELODY

This melody starts out in the natural minor key of B, but 'modulates' (changes) to a major key in the final bar. Keep your ear tuned in to catch this change.

D   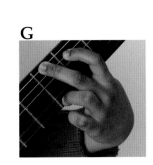 **G**  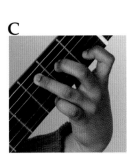 **C**

TOTAL WORKOUT

This piece has it all – chords, single notes and some fiendish rhythms. Set your metronome to a moderate pace and tap out the beat with your foot.

GET THE GROOVE

Clap out the rhythm – remember to check the time signature before you start.

The guitar is perfect for playing with friends. You could play these pieces together or try them as rounds, in which each person starts a bar later than the one before.

RAGGLE TAGGLE GYPSY

This traditional Irish tune should be played at a brisk pace. However, remember to begin slowly and concentrate on getting the notes correct first.

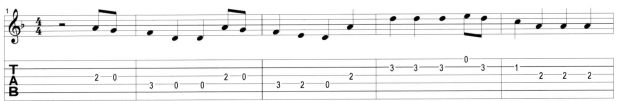

PLAY-ALONG SONGS

BLUES SCALE

Blues is the language of rock 'n' roll. Almost all rock melody lines and tunes can trace their roots back to the blues (*see* page 19), which is based around a very simple scale…

BLUE WITH A FEELIN'

Playing the blues is all about feeling. It is a form of music which first started in the southern states of the USA – the songs of slaves who had been brought from Africa in the 18th century.

Although it can be very emotional, a little technical data is useful for understanding how it works. In the blues scale the third and seventh notes are 'flattened' (down a semitone, or half note – one fret). It is also missing the second and sixth notes where they would be in a 'normal' scale. This makes the blues scale very similar to a minor pentatonic scale (see page 39), but we will come to this soon enough. For now, play the scale below and get the feel of the real blues sound.

Playing with a Capo

Fancy playing in another position on the neck, but still want those lovely ringing tones of the open chords?

It is a cinch with a 'capo' – a device that straps (or clamps) onto the neck and artificially raises the nut. Where you put it is your choice.

Technical Terms

INTERVALS – The space between two notes, measured in length up the scale (1 – 8).

MAJOR AND MINOR THIRDS – A minor third is 'flattened' by a semitone. Compare its sound to a major third by playing one after the other.

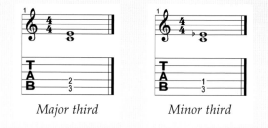

Major third   Minor third

BLUESY SOUNDS

Follow this scale up and down the fingerboard. Start slowly before building up the tempo.

ALTERNATE PICKING

By now, you will be getting pretty handy at using a plectrum. You should know how to strum chords and be a past master at playing scales with one. Here is a technique that will increase your speed and accuracy with the pick…

EASY PICKINGS

It's hard work picking a string in one direction, all the time, especially when it comes to solos. Alternate picking is a great way to pick each string at a higher tempo. It is more accurate and should be used all the time and is extremely useful when it comes to soloing or fast riffs.

1

First of all start picking a certain note on any string. Pick the string firmly downwards, but stop the plectrum as soon as it has plucked the string.

Walking Fingers

Another picking technique is to 'walk' the first two fingers on a string. You can extend this technique to play 'arpeggios'. These are chords in which each note of the chord is sounded on its own, one after the other.

2

The next stroke is an upstroke. Continue playing an alternating down-up-down on the string, making sure to make the strokes evenly. Practise with a metronome.

Start this alternate picking exercise slowly and increase the tempo when you feel comfortable.

EXERCISE 37.1

MAJOR PENTATONIC SCALE

The pentatonic scale is made up of five notes taken from a standard eight-note octave. The major pentatonic scale is a lot like the major scale (*see* page 22) but the fourth and seventh intervals are taken out. So, if you already know the major scale, finding your major pentatonic scale is simple.

Learn Your Scales

Although it may feel like a chore, scales are the building blocks of tunes. Knowing your scales will help you pick out a tune on the guitar and solo like the devil possessed!

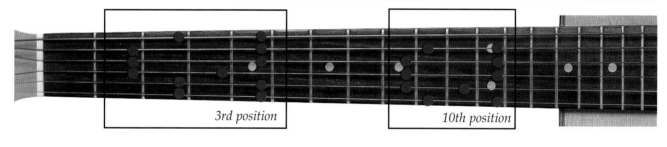

3rd position   10th position

A

This melody is based on the A major pentatonic scale.

EXERCISE 38.1

MINOR PENTATONIC SCALE

The minor pentatonic scale is the crown jewels of scales in the guitar world. Based on the natural minor scale (*see* page 22) – with those added flattened third and flattened seventh notes – this is the scale used by most rock and blues guitarists when soloing.

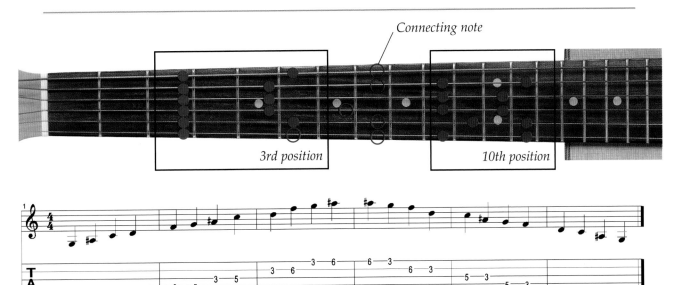

Connecting note

3rd position

10th position

Compare this scale to the blues scale on page 36. You will find that there are a lot of similarities.

Soloing

Mastering this scale in all positions is very important if you want to 'improvise' (make music up as you go along) over rock and blues music. Practise changing positions with runs that use the connecting notes (above).

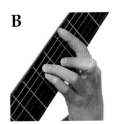

B

Here is a melody based on the minor pentatonic scale. You should also try and construct your own (use the blank tab on page 32).

EXERCISE 39.1

SOLOING TECHNIQUES

Playing the guitar as a solo instrument is really fun, whether you are playing red-hot lead lines on the electric guitar or blistering runs on the classical guitar. There is a whole range of techniques and effects, which you can use when playing solos to increase your speed and dexterity (and flashiness).

CONTROLLED BENDS

1

Bending a string makes the pitch of the note rise. It is used to travel from one note to another smoothly. Pluck a fretted string and while it is still ringing, push the string up towards your head. Practise hitting the notes one fret and two frets above the starting note.

At first, you might find that you need all three fingers to bend a string.

PLAYING RIFFS

1

Practise! Practise! Practise!

It's no lie – practice is the only way to improve your playing. If you want to be really good, you are going to have to put in the time.

Many rock solos and melody lines are built around repeating 'riffs'. One useful technique is to fret the top part of chords on the 1st, 2nd and 3rd strings, in the upper positions, above the 12th fret. Drag the plectrum down across the strings while using your 3rd and 4th finger to add passing notes, or string bends.

VIBRATO

1

Vibrato makes a note 'sing' by pulsing the pitch. It is made by 'wobbling' the fretting finger. Play a note and then push the hand forward of the finger.

2

Quickly swing the hand back, moving from the wrist, and repeat. Can you hear the emotional sound?

SLIDE

1

A slide is a quick way to reach a note during quick runs. If a note is one, two (or even more) frets above the one you are playing, simply slide your fingers up the neck to reach it.

HARMONICS

1

The natural harmonics of a guitar are the pure tones of the strings, without any overtones. Touch any string lightly, directly above the 12th fret.

2

Pluck the string and release your finger from it at the same time. The first harmonic will ring out. You will find others at the 5th and 7th frets.

Artificial Harmonics

The natural harmonics of a string are the places that an open string will produce harmonic tones. You can create 'artificial' or 'forced' harmonics on a fretted string by placing the heel of your picking hand on the strings 12 frets above the fretted note and plucking.

BLUES MELODIES

Now you have learned all about scales, soloing techniques, intervals, and major and minor thirds, it's time to enjoy yourself. Kick back, relax and play some of the tunes on the next two pages. You're nearly there.

PLAYING THE BLUES

The chord progression in the piece below is typical of blues music. It goes from the first note of the scale to a chord based around the fourth note, and then to a chord based around the fifth note of the scale, before returning to the first. Check out the blues scale on page 36.

12-BAR BLUES

Below is a 12-bar blues melody in a 4/4 time signature. The first three bars consist of bluesy chords and the next three bars consist of a melody that you can follow. This will put the blues scale into practice.

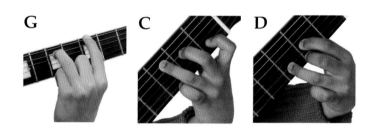

G   C   D

ADVANCED SKILLS

ROCK MELODIES

Congratulations! You have finished the book. By now you should at least have a firm grasp of the basics. Practise the techniques and use the book as reference, flipping back when you need reminding of anything.

PLAY ALONG

Rock melodies are often based around 8-bar blocks. Here are two for you to try. The first play-along song is made up of power chords. Feel free to change them around and make your own melody. On the right are all the chords you will need.

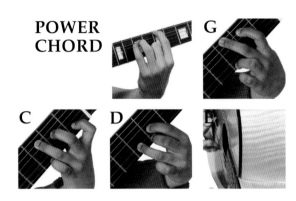

POWER CHORD

G

C   D   E

POWER CHORDS ROCK

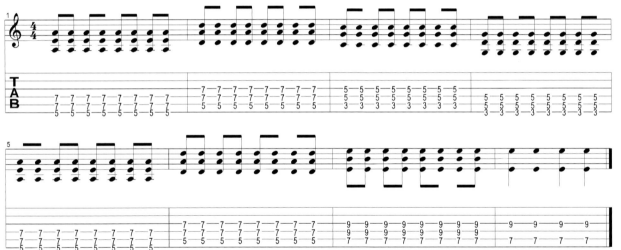

RIFFING ON THE MINOR PENTATONIC

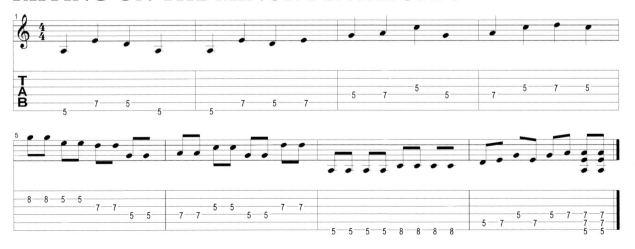

SIGNIFICANT PLAYERS

You could write a whole book on great guitar players. Here are just a few of the glittering stars of the guitar, who have lit up the world of music and changed guitar-playing and guitars forever.

SIX-STRING LEGENDS

The twentieth century was the era when the guitar came into its own as an instrument. As the steel-string guitar grew in popularity, it became a cheap instrument to own and was easy to carry around, as well. People would use it for accompaniment when they got together to sing. Later, with the invention of the electric pick-up, the guitar was transformed into a solo instrument. The six-string gradually became the centre of musical combos and the guitar player the main star.

Charlie Christian

There were other guitar players around who used the new electric pick-up to amplify their sound, but it was Charlie Christian who turned the guitar into a solo instrument. Once a backing instrument only in the largest jazz bands, the six-string was now loud and powerful enough to be a lead instrument like the saxophone. Nobody had ever heard a style like Christian's, when he played with the Benny Goodman Quintet. He also pioneered a new style called 'bebop' jazz.

DJANGO REINHARDT

Django Reinhardt was a master of the acoustic guitar. He was a real mix – born in Belgium to a travelling gypsy family, he grew up in a caravan and played Spanish-influenced jazz in Paris! When he was 18, his hands were burned so badly in a fire that he could only play with his first two fingers. Instead of giving up, Django invented his own way of playing.

Although he couldn't read or write, Reinhardt amazed more refined guitarists, such as Andrés Segovia with his playing technique, often making up or 'improvising' melodies as he went along. His guitar group 'Quintet de Hot Club de Paris' was certainly the hottest thing in Paris in the 1920s and '30s.

BLUES

While jazz was the 'pop' music of the 1920s, '30s and '40s, the blues was more a folksy, country-bumpkin kind of music. Rock 'n' roll burst on the scene in the 1950s, using lots of speeded-up blues tunes. Slowly, the simple, heart-felt melodies and rhythms of blues became more popular.

MUDDY WATERS

McKinley 'Muddy Waters' Morganfield was a blues musician who had a huge influence on young guitar players in the 1960s. People had never heard such music with its loud amplified guitars and a thunderous beat.

JIMI HENDRIX

Nobody, but nobody, had ever before played guitar like Jimi Hendrix. A fantastically talented blues soloist, Jimi's soaring guitar work often saw him play with his teeth, set fire to his guitar or even smash it up. A left-handed player, Hendrix played a right-handed Fender Stratocaster, with the strings strung upside down.

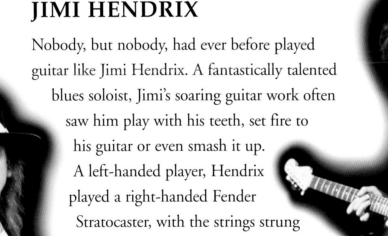

STEVIE RAY VAUGHAN

At age seven, Stevie Ray Vaughan got his first guitar – a toy with only three strings. He learned to play using this guitar and eventually became the world's most influential blues guitarist. Vaughan was famous for his battered 1963 Fender Stratocaster – his favourite – which he had found in an old music shop.

LONG LIVE ROCK 'N' ROLL

As the 1960s rolled on, guitar music changed again, entering the era of rock. Technology improved, and bands were now able to play louder and rock harder. The age of superstar Guitar Heroes was born.

JIMMY PAGE

Perhaps the ultimate Rock God, Jimmy Page was the guitarist for the British band Led Zeppelin – the first world-famous heavy rock band. As well as blistering solos, Page was a very good folk musician and often sprinkled his music with melody lines played on a 12-string guitar. He was also famous for playing his electric guitar with a violin bow. His trademark guitar was a double-necked Gibson SG (left).

ANGUS YOUNG

Dressed in schoolboy's clothes, you cannot mistake Angus Young, the guitarist for the rock band AC/DC. His high-energy style of guitar-playing is hard-rocking and hard-riffing, using a lot of stripped-down power chords. As well as possessing great skill and speed, Young twists the blues to get melody-rich, emotional guitar solos. On stage, he goes crazy, running about and rolling around while playing solos.

POP-TASTIC POP-PICKERS

While rock guitar became bigger and louder, moving to the front of a band, pop guitarists tended to remain in the background – but with great effect.

THE BEATLES

The Beatles were the most successful band ever. A beat combo from Liverpool, they started playing straight rhythm and blues, before changing pop music forever, in the late 1960s. As well as killer melodies, John Lennon and George Harrison cleverly intermingled their guitar parts, to create complex, catchy rhythms. Harrison complemented this with his sweet, country-influenced solos.

BRIAN MAY

Queen are the second-most successful band of all time. Brian May, the guitarist, played off singer Freddie Mercury's theatrical singing with grandiose guitar solos, using lots of effects. May plays a guitar that he built himself with the help of his dad.

47

Custom-made Guitar

The singer and guitarist Prince is one of the most talented, virtuosic pop performers. He mixes a huge range of styles in his playing – usually playing his own custom-made guitars.

ANDRÉS SEGOVIA

It's not all about rock, pop and jazz guitar, though – while the 'rock revolution' was going on, certain musicians distinguished themselves as classical masters. One such guitarist was Andrés Segovia. His expressive style and clever reinterpreting of classical pieces brought this beautiful form of music to the attention of many people. Segovia also did a lot to encourage learners to play the guitar.

GLOSSARY

Apoyando – plucking note, also called the 'rest stroke'.

Arpeggio – a 'broken chord', in which the notes are played in sequence.

barre chord – a chord with the finger used as a 'barre' across the fretboard.

dynamics – how loud or quiet the music should be played.

key signatures – how many sharps and/or flats in a piece.

Legato – played smoothly.

open chord – chords played with open strings ringing.

p-i-m-a – playing with fingers, classical style.

plectrum – a plastic pick for strumming strings.

position – the fret number.

power chord – a three-finger chord.

riff – a repeating pattern, often used in solos.

Staccato – detached notes, played punchily.

strumming – brushing the strings with a plectrum, or a thumb or thumbnail.

tempo – the pace of the music – how fast or slow it goes.

thumbpick – a plastic or metal pick worn on the thumb for fingerstyle playing.

time signature – how many beats, and of what type, in a bar.

Tirando – a plucking stroke, also called the 'free stroke'.

tonic – the main, and first, note of a scale or key signature – also called the 'root' note.

LISTINGS

Contact your local music service to enquire about individual guitar lessons, through the **Federation of Musical Services** (www.thefms.org) or the **European Guitar Teachers Association** (www.egta.co.uk)

http://chordfind.com is a very handy online chord dictionary

www.guitarists.net and http://theguitarresource.com have tons of free resources for guitarists, from beginner to advanced, including finding 'tabbed' music, online lessons, hints and tips, information on other guitarists, links to other guitar websites and this handy electronic tuner program (http://theguitarresource.com/free-online-guitar-tuner).

The website addresses are correct at the time of publishing. However, due to the ever-changing nature of the Internet, websites and content may change. Some websites can contain links that are unsuitable for children. The publisher is not responsible for changes in content or website addresses. We advise that Internet searches are supervised by an adult.